RELEASED FROM CIRCULATION

3 9082 06232990 2

J363.34
ARN

DATE DUE

D1709451

WAYNE PUBLIC LIBRARY
3737 S. WAYNE RD.
WAYNE, MI 48184

APR   1996

Everything You Need to Know About

NATURAL DISASTERS

AND POST-TRAUMATIC STRESS DISORDER

The effects of a natural disaster, such as the strong earthquake that struck Japan, can be devastating.

• THE NEED TO KNOW LIBRARY •

Everything You Need to Know About

NATURAL DISASTERS

AND POST-TRAUMATIC STRESS DISORDER

Mary Price Lee and Richard S. Lee

THE ROSEN PUBLISHING GROUP, INC.
NEW YORK

The authors wish to thank Sheila Kahn Alper for her therapeutic counsel regarding Chapter 6.

To
Nancy and Bill,
Lawrie and John,
Christian and William,
and to Alfio, who brought us together,
with love.

WAYNE PUBLIC LIBRARY
3737 S. WAYNE RD.
WAYNE MI 48184

Published in 1996 by The Rosen Publishing Group, Inc.
29 East 21st Street, New York, NY 10010

Copyright 1996 by The Rosen Publishing Group, Inc.

All rights reserved. No part of this book may be reproduced in any form without permission in writing from the publisher, except by a reviewer.

First Edition

Manufactured in the United States of America

Library of Congress Cataloging-in-Publication Data

Lee, Richard S. (Richard Sandoval), 1927–
    Everything you need to know about natural disasters and post-traumatic stress disorder / Richard S. Lee and Mary Price Lee. — 1st ed.
        p.   cm. — (The need to know library)
    Includes bibliographical references and index.
    ISBN 0-8239-2053-4
    1. Natural disasters—Psychological aspects—Juvenile literature.
2. Post-traumatic stress disorder—Juvenile literature.
[1. Natural disasters—Psychological aspects.   2. Post-traumatic stress disorder.]   I. Lee, Mary Price.   II. Title.   III. Series.
GB5019.L44   1995
603.6′9—dc20   95-13665
                                                                         CIP
                                                                         AC

3 9082 06232990 2

Contents

Introduction

A natural disaster is damage done by Mother Nature that changes your life.

One or more natural disasters can happen almost anywhere in this country. Some areas, such as the West Coast, can have earthquakes and wildfires, but not hurricanes. "Tornado Alley" is the nickname of the flat sections of the Midwest where many of these violent storms occur. Blizzards and ice storms can cripple the whole upper half of North America. Almost any area can flood if there is enough rain. In mountain country, heavy rains can cause flash floods and mud slides.

It pays to be prepared for trouble. But even if you are ready, events such as earthquakes can come as surprises.

Natural disasters can also take their toll psychologically. People often suffer post-traumatic stress disorder (PTSD) after surviving a natural disaster. PTSD is a condition that can cause its victims to have trouble coping with daily life. You will learn more about PTSD and how to deal with it in yourself and in others in this book.

This survivor of an earthquake that hit southern California conducts his business from the sidewalk while workmen repair his much-damaged house.

Dr. David Tribble, Director of the Seismology Station at Loyola University, studies a seismogram of an earthquake that hit the upper Midwest. A seismograph measures and records vibrations within the earth.

Chapter 1

Earthquakes

All the earth below the surface is rock—huge sections of it. These areas are called *tectonic plates*. The cracks where two plates join are *faults*. Faults can run for thousands of miles along *fault lines*. Fault lines are weak areas. Almost all the West Coast of the United States lies along the San Andreas Fault. Here, the Pacific Plate and the North American Plate rub together. When plates are suddenly disturbed, an earthquake results, usually (but not always) along a fault line.

Some scientists think quakes are caused by the pressure on the plates of hot gases beneath them. Others say it is the pull of the tides, or physical changes in the elements that make up the plates. The shock is sudden and sometimes severe. Strong quakes can be felt many miles away from the point where they originate.

Where Quakes Happen

Lower Texas, southern Florida, and the Gulf
Coast are the only places in the United States
where earthquakes do *not* happen. (These are
heavy hurricane areas, however.) Major quake
damage can occur in the Pacific Northwest, California, parts of Utah and Idaho, and the corridor
from Indianapolis to Memphis. Heavy damage can
also take place in coastal South Carolina near
Charleston, along the St. Lawrence River, and on
Cape Cod in New England. Moderate damage can
happen in areas surrounding these places. The
rest of the country would receive only minor
damage.

How Quakes Are Measured

The best-known measurement of earthquakes is
the Richter Scale. Developed in 1935 by Charles
Richter, it measures the energy released by an
earthquake. This energy is called *magnitude.*

You would not feel a quake of 1.0 magnitude. A
2.0 or even a 3.0 quake would do little if any
damage. But each higher number on the scale
means that the earthquake releases *30 times* the
energy of a quake one number below.

Let's say a tremor measuring 1.0 on the Richter
Scale releases one unit of energy. A 2.0 would
release 30 times the energy, or 30 units. A quake
of 3.0 would release 30 times 30, or 900 units. A

quake of Richter magnitude 4.0 would release 30 times 900, or 27,000 units of energy. Although the famous San Francisco earthquake happened 29 years before Richter invented his scale, it has been estimated at 8.25.

San Francisco, April 18, 1906

At 5:12 in the morning, Jesse Cook, a police sergeant, was on street duty. Suddenly, ". . . there was a deep and terrible rumble," the officer said later. The road ahead of him rose and fell in huge waves. "I could see it [the earthquake] actually coming up Washington Street. The whole street was rippling."

The San Francisco earthquake lasted two minutes. The first shock lasted 40 seconds. Two more violent tremors followed. Buildings collapsed. Three thousand acres (490 city blocks) were destroyed. More than 500 people died. Another 250,000 lost their homes. Gas mains burst, starting fires. The water supply was knocked out, so the fires burned out of control for days. Military troops were mobilized to rescue people and halt looting.

An eyewitness described the blazes as "a sea of liquid fire. . . . The sky above seemed to burn at white heat, deepening into gold and orange and spreading into a fierce glare. . . . The fire engulfed a church here; a block of houses there; and a

Thousands of homes were destroyed in the 1994 earthquake that struck Los Angeles, California.

steeple flaring high like a torch toppled and fell in a shower of sparks."

The damage was estimated at $500 million, in the days when an average family could live comfortably on a few dollars a week.

There have been other famous earthquakes in history. An earthquake and tidal wave (tsunami) destroyed Lisbon, Portugal, in 1755. The 1923 Tokyo earthquake was devastating. The 1964 quake that seriously damaged Anchorage, Alaska, was the longest-lasting: seven minutes. Los Angeles had a quake in 1994 that measured 6.6 on the Richter Scale. Scientists say that a serious earthquake will occur along California's San Andreas Fault every 100 to 150 years. Many believe "the big one" is yet to come.

Tsunami: Peril from the Sea

Tsunami means "harbor wave" in Japanese. Tsunamis are also called "killer waves" and "tidal waves," but they have nothing to do with tides. They happen most often in the Pacific Ocean. A tsunami transfers the force of an underwater earthquake to the ocean as waves. Tsunami waves may only be three feet high on the surface, and their crests are far apart. But these waves travel at speeds up to 460 miles an hour and for thousands of miles. Since 1945, more people have been killed by tsunamis than by earthquakes.

The tsunami becomes dangerous when its waves reach shore. In the shallow water, the energy of the waves has nowhere to go but up. The waves grow to as high as 200 feet and strike land with destructive force.

A tsunami was part of the San Francisco earthquake. It reached land about 90 miles north of the city, even as the coast was shaken along the San Andreas Fault. A lighthouse, forests, and many villages were heavily damaged.

The world's greatest tsunami struck the Gilbert Islands in the Pacific in 1958. Its wave was 1,700 feet high at Gilbert Bay and struck land at 100 miles an hour. It broke four-foot-thick trees and swept two thirds of a mile inland.

Islands such as Japan and Hawaii and the coast of mainland China are targets for tsunamis. So is the West Coast of the United States. Warning stations alert coastal residents to their approach, but nothing can be done to control them. Getting out of the way early is the only solution.

If you hear a tsunami warning on the radio, stay away from shore or get to higher ground if you must. *Never go to look at a tsunami.* If you can see it approaching, it is already too late.

How to Prepare for an Earthquake

No one can say when or where a quake will strike. But you can prepare to some extent if you live in an earthquake-prone area. You and your family should have food, water, and medical supplies.

If you are in an earthquake and are indoors (or can safely carry your supplies outside with you), try to have have enough food and water for at least three days. It may take rescue workers that long to take charge of the situation in your area.

If an earthquake wakes you, have sturdy shoes ready to put on. (You could cut your feet on broken glass.) Dress warmly.

If you are indoors, *do not* turn on electricity or gas; you could cause a fire or an explosion. Switch off appliances and gas lines if you know how. A portable cook stove or camp stove is okay outdoors, but never inside.

During the Event

It's almost impossible to think clearly when a quake strikes, but try to remember these tips:

- If you are indoors, stay away from windows.
- Get under something sturdy such as a heavy table or the arch of an inside doorway.
- Put a pillow or a book over your head and neck.
- If you are outside, stay there—and away from power lines, tall buildings, and walls.

What You Can Expect After a Quake

The damage depends on the magnitude of the earthquake. But this is what you can expect to find:

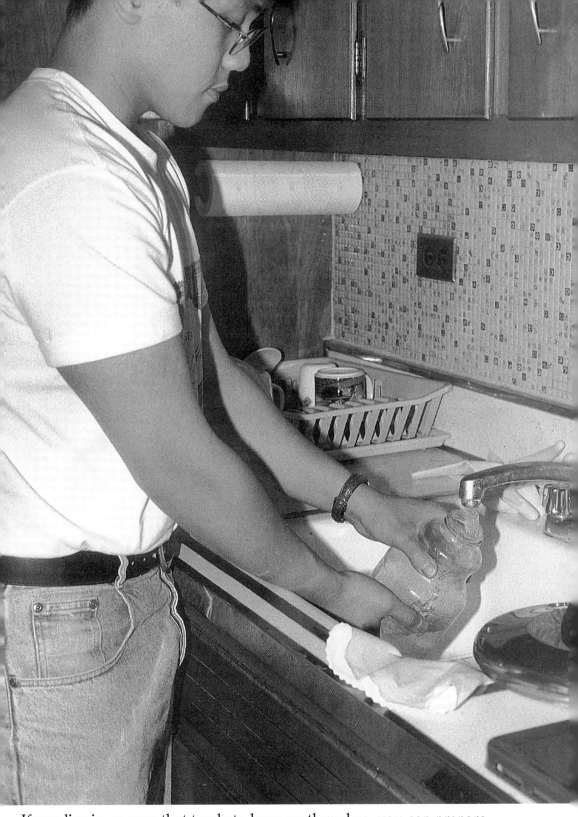

If you live in an area that tends to have earthquakes, you can prepare yourself by always having an ample supply of food and water on hand.

- People who have been killed or hurt
- Badly damaged buildings, roads, bridges
- Fires, downed power lines, and broken gas and water mains
- No electricity, water, or food
- Little or no communications for some time
- Interrupted public services (medical help, etc.)
- No way of getting around except walking (and that can be dangerous).

What to Do and NOT Do After the Rumbling Is Over

Once you come out of your shelter (or stand up if you are outdoors), there is one thing you *should* do and several things you should *not* do.

If you are outdoors or can get outside easily, *do* try to find clear ground and stay there.

If you are trapped indoors, *do not* try to get out. You may be in a spot where pushing against fallen parts of the building could bring more down.

If you are outdoors, you may find fires caused by broken natural gas lines, overturned stoves, and spilled gasoline, kerosene, or solvents. They may flare up from damaged or overturned cars or live electric wires that are touching the ground. Keep away from fires and wires! *Do not* try to put fires out, even if there is water and a hose. If a fire involves gasoline or oil, water will make it worse.

Downed electric wires, flammable liquids, and

other hazards could cause explosions, followed by fire. *Do not* check out things that look strange. *Do not* touch anything. If you are caught inside a building, *do not* turn on gas stoves, house heaters, electric lights, or appliances. If your home or building has natural gas, *do not* light matches.

You may experience aftershocks. These smaller quakes can strike any time. They happen because the first quake has not fully settled the tectonic plates in new positions.

Aftershocks are seldom as strong as the first quake. *But*—and it's a big "but"—aftershocks can collapse buildings, roads, and bridges damaged by the first quake. Aftershocks can start more fires. For that reason, *do not enter any building* after a quake unless someone in command says it's okay. An aftershock may damage it further or bring it down with you inside.

In mountainous areas, the quake and its aftershocks can cause avalanches and, if there is rain, mud slides. Try to find high ground that is clear, not in the shelter of a building.

Water—even public water systems—can quickly become dangerous after a quake. Chemicals and sewage from damaged mains can mix with the water. Do not drink anything that is not bottled or that has not been given to you by a rescue worker.

Be patient. Rescue workers will arrive, although maybe not for a long time.

Chapter 2

Hurricanes and Tornadoes

Hurricanes are sometimes called typhoons. Tornadoes are also called cyclones or twisters. These violent storms are caused by rapid and strong weather changes when cool and hot air masses come together. Winds move in circles at great speed, and the hurricane or tornado itself moves, often in an unpredictable, changing path.

Hurricanes

When Christopher Columbus arrived in the Caribbean Sea, the natives described *hurakans*, or terrible storms. This was news to Columbus, since such storms were unknown in Europe.

Hurricanes begin at sea, over warm water. Since ocean water is warmest in September, that is when most hurricanes start, although they can occur in other months. The hurricanes most likely to reach

the United States form in the Atlantic Ocean. They
tend to strike the Gulf Coast, Florida, and the
lower East Coast. But hurricanes have devastated
New England (the worst one was in 1938) and
have affected inland areas.

Hurricanes are huge storms that blow in circles.
They can cover areas hundreds of miles wide. To
qualify as a hurricane, winds must exceed 74 miles
an hour and can reach 200 miles an hour. The
hurricane itself moves from 10 to 60 miles an hour.
Seen on radar, a hurricane is doughnut-shaped,
with a calm, low-pressure *eye* resembling a
doughnut hole. Swirling around the eye are the
wall clouds. These carry the heaviest rains and
turn at the highest speeds.

Hurricanes can be tracked on radar, but it is
difficult to predict their course. The winds may
grow stronger, or the hurricane may blow itself
out before it reaches land. Life can be very tense
for people living in hurricane country, even with
advance weather warnings.

The Galveston Disaster

No early warnings existed for the 38,000 people
who lived in the Gulf city of Galveston, Texas, on
September 8, 1900. A terrible hurricane struck,
with winds over 120 miles an hour. The low-lying
city was flooded. Bridges to the mainland were
destroyed. Ships were flung out of the harbor; one

If your local radio or TV station announces a hurricane watch, be sure to keep listening for updates and further information.

landed 22 miles inland. By nightfall, when the storm had moved on, more than 7,500 people were dead. This was the highest death toll from any natural disaster in the U.S.

The strongest hurricane wind ever measured was clocked at 183 miles an hour, at Blue Hills, Massachusetts, during the 1938 New England hurricane.

Hurricane Camille (1969) devastated the Mississippi coast. It also continued inland across the Appalachian Mountains, causing flash floods and mud slides. It finally swung out to sea, passing through Norfolk, Virginia.

In 1992, Hurricane Andrew destroyed huge sections of southern Florida. It was the worst storm in the area in more than 60 years and the most widespread, most costly natural disaster in American history. Over 60,000 homes were destroyed. Television brought this monster storm into almost every home in the country.

Hurricanes cannot be controlled. They will continue—anywhere from two to five a season.

"Watch" and "Warning"—and How to Prepare

When forecasters think a hurricane is forming and may become dangerous, they issue a hurricane *watch*. If your radio or TV announces a watch, stay tuned for news. A hurricane *warning* means that the storm is probably going to strike your area. Along with the warning will be instructions as to what to do.

But don't wait until the storm comes to get ready. From June through November, you should:

- Listen regularly for hurricane watches and warnings.
- Know exactly which roads to take inland if you live in low-lying country or in a mobile home.
- Make sure your battery-powered radio has working batteries, and that you have spare batteries for the radio and flashlights.

- Stock up on canned, dried, and sealed foods that don't need to be cooked.
- Make sure your first-aid kit is complete and handy.
- Urge your parents to keep your car's gas tank filled.

If you hear a hurricane *watch*, you should also:

- Keep listening for more news.
- Get ready to leave home, by car or other means, for high ground or for a shelter (your radio will have news).
- Double-check all emergency supplies: See the Disaster Checklist in Chapter 6.
- Be ready to board up or tape windows and sliding glass doors.
- Store all outdoor items (boats, lawn furniture, etc.) indoors.

If the watch is changed to a *warning*, you should:

- Listen *continuously* to the radio.
- Leave home immediately if told to go, especially if you live near shore, on or near a river, or in a mobile home. (Your radio reports may direct you and your family to a nearby shelter, a secure building that can be expected to withstand the storm.)
- If you stay, help your parents board or tape up windows, wedge sliding doors shut, draw all

One way you can prepare yourself for the possibility of a
hurricane is to plan a route to safety.

blinds, and prepare to move valuables and
emergency supplies to the second floor.
- Don't be fooled by the quiet eye of the storm;
  the other half will soon come roaring through.
- Stay away from windows and doors.

Hurricane winds create tremendous pressure on
the side of the house they strike. On the other
side, they create suction. Together, these forces
may be enough to topple the building or, if
windows and doors break, to cause such great air
pressure inside that other windows are blown out
or roofs are blown off. If in doubt, leave ahead of
time.

A Hurricane Experience

Jack's mom and dad heard the watch and the warning. "This house is strong, Jack," his dad said, as they boarded up the downstairs windows together. "We got through two hurricanes before, the last one when you were a baby. We're staying."

"Aren't these warnings worse?" Jack asked.

"Oh, maybe a little. If I hadn't ridden out the other storms, I might be concerned, but we'll make it."

As the storm roared through, the front door blew in. As they scrambled to the second floor, water rushed into the living room. The house swayed and rocked for hours in the night. The eye of the storm came and went. The winds raged again.

By morning, the hurricane was over. Jack and his parents surveyed the damage.

"We're here, anyway," Jack's dad said.

"But not by much," said his mother. "This time, we should have left."

"You're right," Jack's dad said.

Two kinds of people tend to ride out hurricanes: first, those who have survived earlier ones and think they know all about them; second, those who have never experienced one. The latter may ignore warnings because they don't realize what the storm can do. You will never make a mistake by being overcareful with a hurricane. It deserves your respect.

What You May Find Afterward

Whether you stay at home or not, you can expect lots of damage. If you evacuate, you may not get home for days. Roads may not be cleared. Electricity may not be restored. There may be no food. That is why your own supplies are important. Listen to your battery radio for rescue news.

You may see fire damage—the deluge of water from the hurricane will *not* snuff out all fires. But if you find downed wires or are near natural gas or propane tanks, stay away and don't light matches.

Even though water lines may be intact, the water may not be pure because of the heavy rains. Drink the water you have saved, boil other water to drink (with care!), or wait for rescue teams to give you bottled water.

You may find that things you treasure are lost or damaged. Someone in your family or among your friends may have been hurt. People you know may have died. Chapter 6 will help you cope with these problems.

Tornadoes

Tornadoes, like hurricanes, are circular storms formed by the collision of warm and cold air. They, too, move over the land. These storms are very intense and can do great damage. There are minitornadoes and maxitornadoes. Minis are small, with the eye (center) only a few feet across.

Tornadoes can cause widespread damage. This tornado hit the town of Cantrall, Illinois, and destroyed 125 homes as well as two schools.

Maxis can have an eye up to 1 1/2 miles wide. Unlike the eye of a hurricane, a tornado eye is anything but quiet.

Mini or maxi, tornadoes act the same. The cone-shaped storm has swirling winds up to 500 miles an hour in the eye, or *vortex*, the bottom of the cone that reaches the earth. As the tornado (or "twister") touches down, this eye can create tremendous suction as it moves across the ground. It can pull the roofs off houses (or demolish the houses completely) and pick up objects—people, cars, or even livestock—and carry them great distances.

Tornadoes can be just as damaging as

27

hurricanes, but within smaller areas. The lightning from tornadoes can electrocute people and animals. The huge rainfall can cause drowning. It often forms damaging hail.

Not Just in Kansas

In *The Wizard of Oz*, Dorothy and her dog, Toto, were lifted by a twister, only to fall in the Land of Oz. Kansas is prime twister country, but these violent storms can happen almost anywhere. In the summer of 1994, a tragic twister touched down in the town of Limerick, Pennsylvania. An entire family was killed, others were injured, and many homes were damaged—yet eastern Pennsylvania is not twister territory.

Tornadoes occur most often in the South-Central United States, in the flat plains from northern Texas upward to include Oklahoma, Kansas, Arkansas, Missouri, and southern Illinois. The area is often called "Tornado Alley." About 75 percent of all tornadoes happen between March and July, when cool, dry air moving east is most apt to collide with warm, moist air moving north from the Gulf of Mexico.

The Tri-State Twister—Worst of Them All

On March 18, 1925, the Tri-State Twister

appeared in Reynolds County, Missouri. People were fooled because, unlike most tornadoes, this one had no black funnel cloud. It first demolished 90 percent of the town of Annapolis, Missouri, then jumped the Missouri River and totally destroyed Gorham, Illinois. In Murphysboro, the storm, moving on a straight line, wrecked 40 percent of the town and overturned eleven giant steam engines.

Then, in East Frankfort, Illinois, the wind lifted 16 school children from their building, carried them 450 feet and put them down on the ground unhurt—but not a stick or brick of the school remained.

Moving to its third state, Indiana, the twister destroyed the town of Parrish and demolished 25 percent of the buildings in Princeton. Finally, it disappeared.

The Tri-State Twister survived for 3 1/4 hours, traveled 219 miles, killed 689 people, and injured nearly 2,000. It caused $16 *billion* in damages.

What to Do in a Tornado

The rain was pouring down! Sandi's parents had gone to town to do the Saturday shopping, but Sandi had decided not to go.

Later, over the rain, Sandi heard a roaring sound. She looked out the window and saw a black funnel far away. She knew what to do.

"I'll bet it's on TV," she thought—and it was. She didn't stay to watch the picture, but went to the safest spot in the house—in the cellar, under the stairs.

The sound grew louder, like a railroad locomotive passing overhead. The house creaked and groaned. Then things got quiet.

Sandi went back to the TV. The announcer was describing the twister's progress. It was now in a village two miles away.

Her parents came home. They hugged Sandi and cried, so glad everyone was safe. Later, when the rain had stopped, the family looked around. Their garage, about 30 feet across the lawn, was leaning at a crazy angle, but the house had escaped.

Sandi lives in Tornado Alley, so she had been taught in school just what to do in a twister. The teachers had shown the students how to crouch down with their hands over their heads. The students had learned to go to their basement at home, or to an inside wall or inside a closet on the lowest floor of homes with no basement. They had learned to get out of mobile homes and automobiles. They were told not to use the telephone when a twister appears, because the phone can conduct electricity. Because of the lightning, they had learned not to touch bicycles, fences, or other things made of metal. They had learned to stay away from tall trees, flagpoles, and open water.

People in tornado country are also taught that if they're caught outside or in a car they should try to reach a strong shelter. They learn that if they must be outside, they should lie flat in a ditch or crouch next to a building. There is little you can do to get ready for a tornado except to have a basic disaster kit in your house.

What to Expect Afterward

A twister is quirky. It can destroy one home and leave the house next door untouched. Once the storm is over, you can expect anything from severe damage to none at all.

The storm may knock out electricity, but it will not be off for as long as it might in a hurricane, where the damage is widespread. Water systems may be unsafe for a time. If anyone in your family has been injured, or if a friend has been hurt, you will need to cope. Even if you have been spared, you will be affected by the damage others have suffered. Chapter 6 has ideas to help you to cope with the aftermath of a tornado.

Chapter 3

Floods

When it rains gently, rain water soaks into the soil. Hard rain brings down more water than the soil can handle. This extra water flows downward, pulled by gravity, forming streams or creeks. Creeks join one another to form rivers. Rivers may flow for hundreds, even thousands, of miles. Rivers carry water to bays or to oceans.

Floods happen when there is too much water for the ground to absorb. Creeks and rivers cannot carry it away. The water rises higher and higher. It may also move, trying to find its way to a stream or river.

Spring floods take place in colder parts of the country when snow melts. Heavy spring rains alone may cause flooding almost anywhere. The cities along the Mississippi River saw this kind of flood in spring 1993. Sometimes melting snow and spring rains combine to cause a serious flood.

This photo shows a Landsat Thematic Mapper image of the Midwest and the Mississippi River Valley. Healthy vegetation is bright green, and bare soils are tan. One way that the government keeps track of the destruction wrought by floods is using these kinds of maps.

Flash floods can happen even if there's no rain where you are. Water that has piled up elsewhere can come roaring down creeks or rivers, carrying mud, rocks, broken trees, and household goods. On steep mountainsides, heavy rain, floods, and flash floods can cause mud slides heavy enough to carry houses and cars along with them.

Floods are our most common natural disaster. The areas most likely to flood are the Northeast (Maine to North Carolina), Mississippi River area, the Gulf Coast, Texas, and the West Coast. But floods can happen almost anywhere near flowing water. In recent years, floods have devastated parts of Georgia, an area where flooding is rare.

Although floods are caused by nature, some are made worse by man. The disaster in Buffalo Creek, West Virginia, was caused when a dam broke. So was the greatest American flood disaster of all time, the Johnstown Flood.

May 31, 1889

"In an instant the streets became black with people running for their lives. An instant later the flood came and licked them up with one eager and ferocious lap. The whole city was one surging and whirling mass of water, which swept away house after house with a rapidity that even the eye could not follow."

This is what an eyewitness, standing safely on a hilltop, told a *New York Sun* reporter about the Johnstown Flood.

Floods were nothing new to this busy Pennsylvania steel-making city. The town lay in a deep mountain valley where the Stonycreek and Little Conemaugh rivers joined. Spring thaws regularly brought too much water into the town. So it was no surprise that, on May 30, when heavy rains soaked the city, Johnstown began to flood. It rained all night. Water stood five feet deep in the streets by morning.

The South Fork Dam was several miles away and 400 feet higher than Johnstown. It held back the waters of a huge private lake three miles long,

Floods can disrupt entire cities for several days. Heavy rains caused this flood in southern California.

up to a mile wide, and 60 feet deep. The water level grew higher as the rain fell. By morning, water began to leak through the earthen dam, which showed signs of breaking. John Parke, a worker on the dam, saw the danger. Riding his horse to the nearest village, Parke told the telegraph operator to warn Johnstown—but he rode away without hearing the operator shout, "I can't signal! The wires are down!" When the dam burst at 3:10 that afternoon, the huge lake roared toward Johnstown without warning.

The 120-foot wall of water thundered down the Little Conemaugh River. It demolished villages, overturned railroad cars and locomotives, and carried a wall of debris before it. At Johnstown, the debris piled up against a bridge. The trash caught fire as the water engulfed the city of 30,000 people.

Hundreds of people were never found, so the true death toll will never be known. The official number was 2,209. More than 1,500 homes were destroyed. Countless factories were demolished or badly damaged.

Johnstown survived and was rebuilt. It was again severely flooded in 1936. After that, the government spent millions of dollars on flood control and widening the rivers. But the city was flooded again in 1977.

How to Prepare for a Flood

If you live in an area that is subject to flooding, listen to the radio whenever it rains for more than a few hours. *Flood forecasts* will tell you if there is enough melting snow or rainwater to cause local creeks and rivers to overflow. *Flood warnings* will tell you where flooding is taking place and how severe it is. A *flash flood watch* tells you that such a flood can happen. A *flash flood warning* tells you where any flash floods are.

If a flood or flash flood is near you, move to higher ground or evacuate immediately. Your family should have put gas in the car or truck ahead of time and should know the route to take.

In preparing for a flood should your family decide to stay at home rather than evacuate, you should fill the bathtub with water to use later.

As you go, listen to the car radio for news of blocked roads. If you stall or run into high water, get out of the car; it could be carried off by the flood.

If you evacuate, secure the house if there's time. Take loose things like trash cans and outdoor furniture inside. Turn off the gas and electricity.

If you stay, you should have on hand the supplies outlined in Chapter 6. You should also fill a bathtub with water to use later. Your family may need to put up sandbags, plywood, and plastic sheeting to protect your home from flood damage. They should also know how high your home is above any creeks, streams, or rivers that could flood. If your home is 10 feet above water level and floods are expected to crest at 15 feet above normal, you may find five feet of water in your home.

What to Do Afterward

If you have evacuated, stay away from flooded areas until you are told by rescue workers that it's okay to return. Don't enter your home if the water is above the first floor. Indoors, use flashlights, not risky lanterns. Don't use water until you are told it is safe. Avoid foods that have been touched by flood water, even if they look all right. Don't touch gas lines, electric wires, or fuse boxes. Leave these for utility workers to inspect and repair.

You may find major flood damage in your home. It could be weeks or months before things are back to normal. The whole community may be struggling to recover from the damage and losses of the flood.

Chapter 4

Wildfires

This chapter discusses wildfires, but keep in mind that *home* fires are a far greater danger. The Federal Emergency Management Agency (FEMA) says that home fires have killed more Americans since 1900 than all our wars in the same period.

Whether you and your family live in a tiny city apartment or a sprawling farmhouse, following these simple safety rules will help prevent home fires:

- Install smoke detectors. Test batteries weekly. Clean detectors regularly. Change batteries yearly.
- Plan ahead how each family member will escape from a home fire, using two exits from every room (if practical).
- If your area has 911 emergency calling, know how to use it. If not, paste the fire department phone number by every telephone.

Although home fires are a greater danger, wildfires can be terrifying.

- Store flammable materials in safe containers outside the home.
- Promptly dispose of rags used with paints or solvents, old newspapers, paint cans, and other materials that can burn.
- Keep a fire extinguisher handy, and be sure everyone knows how to use it. (*Never* use water on an electrical fire.)
- Regularly check stoves, fireplaces, and heaters for cleanliness and safe operating condition.
- Do not use frayed electric wiring, and do not overload wall sockets or extension cords.
- Know where gas and electricity shutoffs are so you can close them in an emergency.

- If a small fire breaks out, try to extinguish it, *But call the fire department anyway*—do not wait! Get everyone off the premises at once.

Wildfires—Western Menace

In July, 1994, 14 firefighters were killed battling a wildfire on Colorado's Storm King Mountain. It was one of America's worst firefighting disasters. High winds not in the forecasts advanced the flames faster than some firefighters could retreat.

"I have strong legs and fast feet," said one firefighter who survived. "I simply outran the fire uphill. I crested the hill and headed down the other side. [Fire] doesn't travel downhill quite as quickly, so I was able to get out of the intense heat."

The massive blaze was one of 31 wildfires that burned in nine Western states that summer. More than 7,700 firefighters battled the fires. Flames devoured 160,000 acres. In 1988, wildfires in Yellowstone National Park area blazed as high as 300 feet, burning out more than a million acres. Fires in the Idaho panhandle and western Montana killed 78 people and consumed three million acres.

In the East, the wet climate, rolling ground, and smaller forests make wildfires less menacing. Lack of rain, high temperatures, and large forest areas create the high-risk conditions that can cause wildfires.

Whether a wildfire is set, an accident, or the result of lightning, which causes 35 percent of wildfires, the destruction can be total and the flames relentless. Wildfires usually destroy open land, but in populated areas in dry, hot weather with little rain, the stage can be set for the destruction of homes and whole neighborhoods.

If you live where wildfires can sweep through woodland or even the thin forests of a suburban neighborhood, the risk is real. What can you do?

Stay Tuned

If you live in Arizona, California, Colorado, Idaho, Montana, Nevada, New Mexico, Oregon, western Texas, Utah, Washington State, or Wyoming, be alert for wildfire news in fire season (May through October in most areas). If summer weather is extremely hot and dry, other sections of the country can also have wildfires.

Be sure your parents keep the car filled with gas at all times (service stations may close in an emergency). Every morning, listen to radio or TV news or to a weather radio. If you hear fire news, you will be alerted about what to do or where to go.

The Only Preparation Is Escape

Your parents may have built your home with fire-resistant materials and created a safety zone

When you evacuate your house, make sure you turn off all utilities and lock the doors.

around the house with no vegetation that could burn. This may help in the case of local brush fires. But if you hear news of a forest fire or wildfire the *only* thing to do is get out. If authorities say to go, don't delay—and *do not* believe you can save your home by staying behind and hosing it down. Even without high winds, a wildfire can consume everything in its path.

When you escape a wildfire:

- Take the routes you are given on the radio. Avoid shortcuts or other roads; they may be closed.
- Take your emergency supplies with you (see Chapter 6).
- Lock the house. If there is time, turn off all utilities.
- Pack only essentials—people are more valuable than things.
- Try to tell other family members where you are going.

What to Expect Afterward

If a wildfire reaches your home, you may be faced with severe damage or a total loss. Losing your home, or dealing with heavy damage is upsetting. Chapter 6 contains tips for coping with these terrible experiences.

Chapter 5

Blizzards and Ice Storms

D id you know that an erupting volcano once caused 12 months of frost and snow even in warm places like Florida?

The year 1816 was the coldest in history. Ice storms and frost killed crops and kept farmers from making a living. It was all caused by a volcano on Indonesia's remote Isle of Sumbawa. The volcano spewed volcanic ash that circled the earth and blocked out most of the sunlight. Temperatures plummeted.

This freakish weather never happened again. But great blizzards and bitter weather have always been part of America's heritage.

The Blizzard of 1888

This famous blizzard blanketed the northeastern United States, an area where blizzards often occur.

The northern half of the United States and all of Canada are subject to blizzards.

(They can also happen anywhere across the northern half of the country.) The storm buried towns and villages. The snow topped four feet, but the dramatic sights were the 30- to 40-foot drifts.

At many houses, snows reached the second floor. People who dared leave their homes tunneled through drifts to get out. Many did not return; they lost their way and died of exposure. Those who stayed home had little food or heat. More than 200 people perished in New York City during the Blizzard of '88.

Violent snowstorms still rage. From 1896 to 1990, 428 people died because of bitter weather.

What Is a Blizzard?

Blizzards develop in North America because cold, dry air from Canada sweeps down to meet warm air from the far-off Pacific Ocean. These two forces create a storm system. Because of the low winter temperatures, the result is blowing snow, not heavy rain.

For a snowstorm to qualify as a blizzard, the temperature must fall to 20 degrees Fahrenheit or below. The wind must blow at 35 miles an hour or higher. If these conditions are met, the thick, blowing snow of a blizzard becomes very serious.

Blizzards can prevent you from seeing more than six feet ahead. Ground and sky become one swirling mass of white. If you are outdoors, you can lose your sense of direction and become lost. You can suffer frostbite. When you add the high winds to the low temperatures, you get a wind chill factor that makes a blizzard feel far colder than it actually is.

Blizzard snow may be beautiful to watch, but it can spell major trouble. If you drive, it's almost impossible to see the road, even with your own and other cars' headlights. You can easily become snowbound for many dangerous hours. If you are at home, you may lose electricity. When the current goes out, so may your heat. You could be marooned in your home for several days if the blizzard is severe.

Blizzard Survival

First, listen for weather reports on radio or TV. The five-day forecasts will allow you to brace for the storm. The radio may alert you to a winter storm *watch*, meaning a possible storm. If you hear a storm or blizzard *warning*, snow is on the way. The blizzard warning means business! The blinding snow and wind chill will get your attention.

In ski resort areas such as Colorado, or in any mountain country with heavy snowfall, dangerous avalanches can strike. An avalanche is a mass of snow that breaks loose and slides down a mountain. Skiers and motorists in avalanche areas are at high risk.

Austin knew what to do when he heard the blizzard warning on the radio. He and his parents had been through many bad storms in their New England home.

"I'll bring the shovels in the house and get rock salt for the front door path," he told his parents.

Mom checked the emergency supplies. She filled a bathtub with extra water, in case the heat went off and the water pipes froze. She also had lots of sealed food that didn't need heating. ("Even cold tuna beats starving," Austin thought.)

They knew that if the electricity failed their oil burner wouldn't turn on. "I'll bring in enough wood for a week," Dad said. "The wood will stay dry, and we'll keep the fireplace going all the time. Austin, you can even read by firelight. Abraham Lincoln did!"

Austin's family were prepared for the worst. They had food, warm clothes, bed covers, sleeping bags, and emergency water. They could keep in touch with their battery-powered radio. They all knew there was no place like home in a blizzard!

When it came, it hit hard. As night approached, their electricity did *fail. "It's a lights-out, bitter cold night for us," Mom commented. But Austin didn't mind. He really* could *read by the firelight.*

Chapter 6

Coping with a Disaster and Post-traumatic Stress Disorder

Planning Ahead

This checklist is adapted from "Are You Ready?", published by the U.S. Federal Emergency Management Agency (FEMA).

DISASTER SUPPLIES CHECKLIST
- At least three gallons of bottled water per person (one per day) in sealed plastic containers (several times this amount of water should be stored for floods, hurricanes, and blizzards)
- Canned foods: fruits, vegetables, meat, milk (or milk powder), beans, etc. that do not need cooking
- Sealed or packaged foods that do not need refrigeration, such as granola bars, cookies, and dried fruit—altogether, enough food for two weeks

- A hand-operated can opener and bottle openers
- Flashlights and battery-operated radio with extra batteries. (A battery-powered weather radio that receives only continuous weather reports is sold in electronics stores for about $20.)
- Candles and matches (protected against moisture)
- A heat source (camp stove or canned heat)—use with care!
- Blankets and sleeping bags
- Rain gear and extra clothing, including sturdy shoes and (in cold conditions) warm outerwear
- Credit cards and extra cash
- A complete first-aid kit (buy the best)
- A list of medications, doctors' telephone numbers, and other medically related family information
- Extra car keys
- Spare eyeglasses (if you or family members wear them)
- Toilet paper, paper towels, plastic trash/garbage bags
- Valuables (personal papers, jewelry, etc.)

THIS IS ONLY THE MOST BASIC LIST FOR ANY DISASTER EMERGENCY. YOUR SUPPLIES SHOULD BE KEPT TOGETHER, IN AN ACCESSIBLE PLACE. EVERY

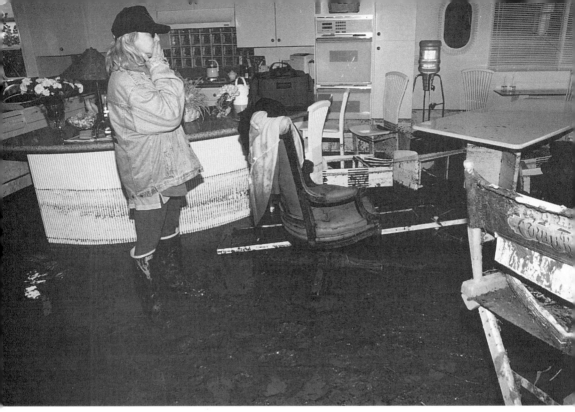

Feelings of depression and despair are common in
survivors of natural disasters such as floods.

MEMBER OF THE FAMILY SHOULD KNOW WHERE
THESE SUPPLIES ARE KEPT. IF POSSIBLE, TAKE THEM
WITH YOU IF YOU MUST LEAVE HOME IN A DISASTER
EMERGENCY.

After Disaster Strikes

Cover the basics. Are you all right? Is your
family together? Is anyone hurt? How can you
help?

Later, find out how others are. What about
neighbors? Your friends?

Also later, look at the physical damage. How is

your home? Your street? Your school? What was lost, damaged?

You have been through a "time-stopping" event. At first you may feel numb and unreal. That is natural. You have suffered genuine loss. Getting over what happened will take time. How long will depend on:

- how serious the disaster was for everyone
- how serious it was for you, your family and friends
- how positive your attitude is
- what bad things, if any, happen *after* the event.

Your home may have been damaged or even destroyed. Many of the things you treasure may have been lost. You may have to live in a shelter, with its discomfort and loss of privacy. Your school may have been damaged. You may not know for some time if all your friends are okay.

You may have vivid memories or even bad dreams about what happened—or you may not recall everything about the disaster. You may feel sad. These are all normal reactions. They are part of what is now called post-traumatic stress disorder (PTSD).

Defining PTSD

Post-traumatic stress disorder is a psychological disorder that can make its victims have difficulty dealing with everyday life. Recognized first in war veterans, PTSD has now been found in victims of nearly any traumatic incident, including natural disasters. Studies show that about one in four people develop PTSD after a major disaster.

The people most likely to develop PTSD are those who have difficulty acknowledging or expressing their emotions. A victim of PTSD experiences a number of emotions ranging from numbness to anger. You may feel disoriented, guilty for having survived when others perhaps did not. You may even be depressed. You have lost things that are important to you. Your life may have been totally disrupted. You and your family may not feel in control of your lives and may not for a long time. Your parents may have no jobs to go to and no income for a while. Someone you know may have been hurt or even killed. You and your family cannot tell how things will turn out.

Despite not knowing what will happen, and the fact that you are dealing with all sorts of difficult emotions, you can begin recovering from the shock by taking things one step at a time.

First, allow yourself to feel whatever emotions are tumbling around inside. Then, work on getting rid of the anger you feel. Holding anger in can make you depressed. Think of yourself putting your anger in a great big balloon and "letting it go."

Get enough sleep, but don't be surprised if

sleeping well takes time. Think about pleasant memories or a funny TV show you have seen. You may have trouble remembering things, especially about the disaster. Your memory will improve.

You may feel guilty, as though you were to blame for what happened. You were *not*, but many people make the mistake of taking personal responsibility for negative events. They feel that what they did or did not do during the event was wrong. This only adds to depression.

People who go through disasters often fear that it will happen again. You may dream about the event. Some survivors of the Buffalo Creek floods in West Virginia had nightmares about water chasing them. They could not trust the natural world. It took a long time for them to recover.

Sometimes schoolwork takes a beating, and grades go down. These, too, are things you can overcome.

Watch out for a tendency to take unusual risks. Without realizing it, you may feel that, since you have survived this terrible scene, you won't be hurt by anything. But, whatever the reason, taking chances is *not* a good move when you're trying to recover from a traumatic event.

If you feel, as many people with PTSD do, that you simply cannot cope with what has happened, speak to a counselor or a therapist who will help you deal with the emotions brought on by the trauma.

Coping Strategies—Bad and Good

There are *bad* coping strategies. It is easy to fall into their trap. Mental health workers who have studied the effects of natural disasters on young people say that it is often hard to avoid negative ways of coping. They include:

Distraction. It may take a real effort not to be distracted from your goal of getting your life together again.

Withdrawal. If you are frightened and sad about what has happened, it may seem natural to keep to yourself. It is easier to retreat than to face the future. But you must face it some day. Try to do it now, one step at a time.

Blaming yourself. Blaming yourself for something you did not cause is negative thinking. It can make you depressed. Even if there were things you could have done during the disaster, it is simply not possible to think and act perfectly under terrible conditions.

Blaming others. Even if you think others in your family acted unwisely, the disaster is not their fault. Your family probably did the best they could.

Wishful thinking. "If only..." is another way of hiding from reality. Wishing the disaster had not happened may give a sense of comfort—but the comfort does not last because the bad things really *did* happen.

Regulating your emotions. You have suffered a loss, perhaps a serious one. You must face it. Bottling up your emotions can be bad for you as you try to cope. You must acknowledge and work through these emotions if you are to get over your loss. You can't change what happened, but you can control how you deal with the emotions that it causes:

- *Denial.* Wishfully thinking that the event never happened.
- *Anger.* Once you accept the fact that something bad did happen, you may be angry about what it did to you. Let off steam, but do not be angry at other people. Work through your anger, then let it go.
- *Depression.* Feeling down about what has happened to you is natural. It will take hard work to get through it. You may need help from professional counselors.
- *Acceptance.* The final stage. Once you accept things as they really are, you can begin to make life better, one step at a time.

There are three good, positive coping skills. You should try to put them all to work for you. They are:

Solving problems. You and your family will have many problems to face after a disaster. To keep from becoming part of the problem, work to

be part of the solution. Ask *exactly* how you can
help. Maybe you can sort through damaged
belongings, boil water for drinking, baby-sit your
little brother, or care for a neighbor's child. By
helping others to solve problems, and by keeping
busy, you are being both helpful and positive.
Tackle things one at a time. Do not try to do too
much too quickly. You will feel overwhelmed.

 ~ **Rebuilding your thinking.** It will not be easy
to think clearly and positively about the future. It
is hard to overcome negative thoughts and
memories of the disaster, and you may need outside
help in rebuilding your thinking. But you should
try to think about getting life back to normal.

To help rebuild your thinking:

- Get counseling if you need it.
- Look at the positive side. You are alive. You are
  going to be all right. You can help make things
  better.
- Try not to feel sorry for yourself. You are not
  the only person with problems. Many others
  may be much worse off than you.
- Remember, you can be useful to others.

 ~ **Reaching out to others.** You will help others
in your family just by showing your support.
"Building a bridge" to family and friends will help
you to recover from the damage everyone has
suffered. Find out what has happened to your
friends. Help them recover. Let them help you,

even if it is only by being your friend. Doing
things for others will take your mind off yourself.

What Happens Next?

As you begin to recover, there may be setbacks
for everyone in the family. It may be it hard to get
life back to normal. When things go wrong, you
may relive the disaster and blame *it* for what is
happening. If you slip back a step, you must try
once more to get ahead.

Only a small number of people suffer lasting
effects of a disaster and PTSD. Most recover
completely. If, however, you find that you are
having difficulty recovering, there are people you
can talk to. Check with your parent, teacher,
guidance counselor, or doctor to find group
therapy meetings for PTSD. If there are none in
your area, you might try a private counseling
session with a licensed therapist. Recovering from
disaster just takes time; how much time depends
largely on how badly your life was upset.

Remember, you will get your life together.
Things will be better. Time is one friend. A
positive outlook is another. Believe in yourself and
your ability to help yourself. In your mind's eye,
picture yourself smiling and doing well. The more
you "see" yourself happy, the happier you will
actually become.

Where to Go for Help

If there is a serious disaster in your area, you can get help and emotional counseling from one or more of these organizations and agencies: the American Red Cross, the Salvation Army, the Federal Emergency Management Agency (FEMA), and state, county, and local government and service organizations.

Your local chapter of the American Red Cross can supply complete disaster preparation information, including "Are You Ready? Your Guide to Disaster Preparedness." The American Red Cross and the Canadian Red Cross Society (613-739-3000) can also provide additional booklets to help you prepare for any disasters that may occur where you live.

If there is no Red Cross office near you, write to the Federal Emergency Management Agency, P.O. Box 70274, Washington, DC 20024, Att: Publications. Ask for a copy of "Are You Ready?" It also lists many other publications that deal with specific disasters. These publications are free. Some are available in Spanish. You can also write to Canadian Red Cross Society, 1800 Alta Vista Drive, Ottawa, ON K1G 4J5 for more information.

Glossary—*Explaining New Words*

aftershock   Minor quake following the shock of a main earthquake.

avalanche   Large mass of material, usually snow, moving swiftly down a mountainside or over a cliff.

cyclone   Windstorm that whirls around a center of low atmospheric pressure, advancing at 20 to 30 miles per hour.

eye   Area of moderate calm and fair weather at the center of a hurricane.

fault   Fracture of the crust of the earth where tectonic plates do not meet.

flash flood   Sudden rush of water down a narrow gully or over a sloping surface, caused by heavy rain.

magnitude (Richter scale)   Open-ended logarithmic scale for expressing the strength of an earthquake in terms of the energy released by it.

tectonic plates   Large sections of rock beneath the earth's surface; when disturbed, an earthquake results.

tornado   Violent windstorm occurring over land, characterized by a long, funnel-shaped cloud that extends to the ground.

twister   Tornado.

vortex (tornado)   Whirling mass of air that forms the center of a tornado.

For Further Reading

Alth, Charlotte and Max. *Disastrous Hurricanes and Tornadoes*. New York: Franklin Watts, 1981.

Armbruster, Ann, and Taylor, Elizabeth A. *Tornadoes*. New York: Franklin Watts, 1989.

Beattie, Melody. *Codependent No More*. New York: Hazelden/Harper Collins, 1987.

Brindze, Ruth. *Hurricanes—Monster Storms from the Sea*. New York: Athenaeum, 1973.

Dudman, John. *The San Francisco Earthquake—Great Disasters*. New York: Bookwright Press, 1988.

Erikson, Jon. *Violent Storms*. Blue Ridge Summit, PA: Tab Books, Inc., 1988.

Fradin, Dennis Brindell. *Disaster! Hurricanes*. Chicago: Children's Press, 1982.

Gilford, Henry. *Disastrous Earthquakes*. New York: Franklin Watts, 1981.

Goetz, Delia. *Rivers*. New York: William Morrow & Co., 1969.

Pringle, Lawrence. *Natural Fire, Its Ecology in Forests*. New York: William Morrow & Co., 1969.

Radlauer, Ed and Ruth. *Earthquakes*, Chicago: Children's Press, 1987.

Stein, R. Conrad. *The Story of the Johnstown Flood*. Chicago: Children's Press, 1984.

Index

About the Authors
Richard S. Lee is an advertising writer and free-lance author. Mary Price Lee is a former educator, now a free-lance writer. The Lees have written many books for The Rosen Publishing Group, including *Caffeine and Nicotine* and *Drugs and Codependency* for The Drug Abuse Prevention Library.

Photo Credits
Cover by Michael Brandt; pp. 2, 7, 8, 12, 27, 33, 35, 40, 46, 52 © AP/Wide World Photos; pp. 16, 21, 24, 37, 43 by Kim Sonsky.